Explore!
ANGLO-SAXONS

Jane Bingham

First published in Great Britain in 2017 by Wayland

Dewey number 942'.01-dc23
ISBN 978 0 7502 9734 9
Library ebook ISBN 978 0 7502 9557 4
10 9 8 7 6 5 4 3 2 1

Wayland
An imprint of Hachette Children's Group
Part of Hodder & Stoughton
Carmelite House
50 Victoria Embankment
London EC4Y 0DZ

An Hachette UK Company
www.hachette.co.uk

www.hachettechildrens.co.uk

A catalogue record for this title is available from the
British Library

Printed and bound in China

Produced for Wayland by

White-Thomson Publishing Ltd
www.wtpub.co.uk

Editor: Izzi Howell
Designer: Clare Nicholas
Picture researcher: Izzi Howell
Illustrations for step-by-step: Stefan Chabluk
Proofreader: Izzi Howell
Wayland editor: Annabel Stones

Picture acknowledgements:
The author and publisher would like to thank the
following agencies and people for allowing these
pictures to be reproduced:

Cover (top left) Vespasian Psalter/Wikimedia; (top right)
portableantiquities/Wikimedia; (bottom left) Aiwok/Wikimedia;
(bottom right) Colin Young/Thinkstock; (other cover elements)
Daniel H.Haigh/Wikimedia, Zaptik/Shutterstock, artform/
Shutterstock, Andrey_Kuzmin/Shutterstock; title page (left)
RMAX/iStock; (right) Meister des Book of Lindisfarne/
Wikimedia; p.4 Hulton-Deutsch Collection/Corbis; p.5 (top)
Nick Ledger/JAI/Corbis; (bottom) Eddie Keogh/Reuters/
Corbis; p.6 (left) Dorling Kindersley/Thinkstock; (right)
meunierd/Shutterstock; p.7 (top) Pavel Klasek/Shutterstock;
(bottom) Stefan Chabluk; p.8 Ted Spiegel/Corbis; p.9 (left)
Bede's Life of St Cuthbert/Wikimedia; (right) David Benton/
Shutterstock; p.10 Photos.com/Thinkstock; p.11 (top) Photos.
com/Thinkstock; (bottom) Photos.com/Thinkstock; p.12 (left)
Colin Young/Thinkstock; (right) Stefan Chabluk; p.13 Stefan
Chabluk; p.14 MS Cott/Wikimedia; p.15 (top) Costumes of All
Nations (1882) Albert Kretschmer, painters and costumer to the
Royal Court Theatre, Berin, and Dr. Carl Rohrbach/Wikimedia;
(bottom) West Stow; p.16 West Stow; p.17 (top) Pierluigi De
Vecchi ed Elda Cerchiari, I tempi dell'arte/Wikimedia; (bottom)
Wikimedia; p.18 Arthur Rackham/Wikimedia; p.19 (top) Joseph
Martin Kronheim/Wikimedia; (bottom) Meister des Book of
Lindisfarne/Wikimedia; p.20 Science Photo Library; p.21
(top) Fotokostic/Shutterstock; (bottom) RMAX/iStock; p.22
Jononmac46/Wikimedia; p.23 (top) Andrewrabbott/Wikimedia;
(bottom) Vespasian Psalter/Wikimedia; p.24 Helen Stratton/
Wikimedia; p.25 (top) Fine Art Photographic Library/Corbis;
(bottom) John W. Schulze/Wikimedia; p.26 Wikimedia; p.27
(top) Myrabella/Wikimedia; (bottom) GraphicaArtis/Corbis;
p.28 (top) portableantiquities/Wikimedia; (bottom) Johnbod/
Wikimedia; p.29 Arena Photo UK/Shutterstock.

Contents

Who were the Anglo-Saxons?

Around the year 400CE, bands of warriors began to launch surprise raids on England. Gradually, they gained control of most of the country. These people became known as the Anglo-Saxons and they ruled England for over 500 years.

Invaders and settlers

The first Anglo-Saxons to arrive in England claimed land by force, but they were soon followed by settlers who lived as farmers. The Anglo-Saxon people were Angles and Saxons from Angeln and Saxony (modern-day Germany), and Jutes from Jutland (modern-day Denmark). Their new lands became known as 'Angle-land' or the land of the Angles. Over time, this name changed to 'England'.

Fierce warrior chiefs led the Anglo-Saxons in their raids on England.

4

Anglo-Saxon England

Most Anglo-Saxon people lived in villages and worked as farmers. The villagers worked for their local lord, or thane, and the thanes were loyal to their king. By the year 600CE, England was divided into powerful kingdoms and in 927 the country was united under a single king. The Anglo-Saxon kings fought off many attacks by Viking invaders from Denmark. Their power came to a sudden end in 1066, when England was conquered by the Normans from France.

Some impressive buildings survive in England from Anglo-Saxon times. This underground crypt is part of a church at Lastington in Yorkshire.

Archaeologists have found some amazing objects buried in the ground. This is part of the Staffordshire Hoard, which was discovered in 2009.

How do we know?

The Anglo-Saxon people left all sorts of evidence of their way of life. Many buildings have survived, and archeologists have found a range of objects, from tools and cooking pots to weapons and jewellery. There are also some fascinating written records, including illustrated manuscripts. All these sources show us how people lived in England a thousand years ago.

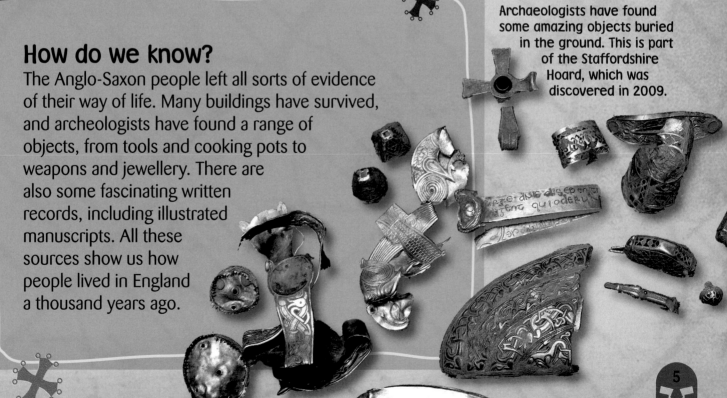

Anglo-Saxon England

The first Anglo-Saxon raids on England began around 380CE. At that time, England was part of the Roman Empire. The Romans had conquered Britain in 43CE, but by the 380s many parts of their Empire were under attack from raiders.

The Anglo-Saxons take over

Around the year 400, Roman soldiers in Britain were ordered to return to Rome to defend their capital city. The last Roman soldiers left Britain in 410, leaving the British people without an army to fight off invaders. Gradually, the Anglo-Saxons took control of southeast England. Some Ancient Britons retreated to Scotland, Wales and Cornwall. But most stayed in England and accepted the Anglo-Saxons as their rulers.

Roman soldiers defended Britain from invaders until the Roman army were sent back to Rome.

Roman Empire

This map shows the Roman Empire at its largest. Britain was the most northern land in the Empire.

Searching for land

There wasn't enough farming land to go round in Angeln, Saxony and Jutland, the homelands of the Angles, Saxons and Jutes. By the 380s, people were growing restless and so some of them travelled to England in search of new land.

Saxony was covered by mountains and forests, so the Saxons needed more farming land.

Anglo-Saxon kingdoms

By the year 600, thousands of Anglo-Saxons had settled in southeast England. The country was divided into kingdoms ruled by warrior kings. Kent, Wessex and East Anglia were all important kingdoms, but the largest and most powerful were Northumbria and Mercia.

This map shows the routes taken by the Anglo-Saxon tribes and the main kingdoms that they set up in England. Today, Jutland is part of Denmark, and Angeln and Saxony are both parts of Germany.

Northumbria

Jutland

Mercia

Angeln

East Anglia

Saxony

Wessex   Kent

Areas settled by the Anglo-Saxons

Angles

Jutes

Saxons

Anglo-Saxons and Danes

B y the late 700s, England was a largely peaceful country under the rule of the Anglo-Saxons. But then fierce invaders began to arrive on English shores. The invaders were Vikings from Denmark, Norway and Sweden. Most of them came from Denmark so the Anglo-Saxons called them 'the Danes'.

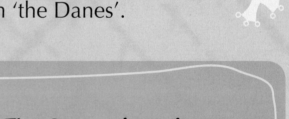

The Danes invade

In 865, the Danes launched a full-scale invasion of England. Within five years, they had won control of most of the country, but then King Alfred of Wessex decided to fight back. In 878, Alfred's army won a great victory at the Battle of Edington.

This Anglo-Saxon gravestone shows violent Danish warriors. The Danes were greatly feared by the Anglo-Saxon people.

Alfred and the Danelaw

After Alfred's victory, the Danes agreed to divide England in two. There was a Danish ruler in the northeast, while Alfred was king in the southwest. Each half of the country had its own laws, and the Danish half became known as the 'Danelaw'. The Danes ruled the Danelaw until 937, when they were defeated by Alfred's grandson, Aethelstan, at the Battle of Brunanburh.

This statue shows King Alfred of Wessex. After his death, he became known as King Alfred the Great.

A struggle for power

King Aethelstan and his descendants ruled the whole of England, but they still had to fight off Danish attacks. In 991, King Aethelred paid the Danes large sums of money, known as the Danegeld, in return for a promise to stay away. However, this plan did not succeed for long. The Danes invaded again in 1012, and for much of the following 30 years England was ruled by Danish kings.

This illustration shows Aethelstan, the first king of England, presenting a book to St Cuthbert. Aethelstan encouraged learning and supported the leaders of the Christian Church.

A warrior's letter

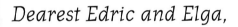

This is a fictional letter from a warrior in King Alfred's army. He is writing to his children on the night before the Battle of Edington.

Dearest Edric and Elga,

I send you fondest greetings. I like to think of you both safe at home while I restring my bow, ready for battle tomorrow.

We have been treated kindly by the people here. Even King Alfred himself – disguised as a common soldier – was invited to stay in a poor woman's home. But when she left him in charge of cooking her cakes, Alfred was so busy with his battle plans that he let them burn. You should have heard the way she shouted at the king!

If we win tomorrow, Alfred has great plans. He will grant some land to the Danes, but the rest of England will be ruled by him. He will make good laws and build churches and forts, as well as ships to protect our coast. Truly, he will be King Alfred the Great!

Now I have to sleep so I am ready for battle. Tomorrow, we will decide the future of England!

I pray to God to keep you safe from the Danes.

Your loving father, Oswin

The letter on this page has been written for this book. Can you write your own letter, from Oswin's son or daughter, telling your father about your life at home? Use the facts in this book and in other sources to help you write about life in an Anglo-Saxon village.

Make an Anglo-Saxon helmet

Anglo-Saxon warriors were sometimes buried in ships. In 1939, the remains of a ship burial were discovered at Sutton Hoo in Suffolk. Inside the ship were a helmet and sword and other precious possessions. You can make you own warrior's helmet, based on the famous helmet found at Sutton Hoo.

You will need:

bendy card measuring around 25 cm x 19 cm (the front of a cereal packet works well)

ruler

pencil

scissors

crayons

elastic

1 Use your ruler and pencil to draw a vertical line halfway across the top of the card. Then draw a horizontal line halfway down the side of the card. Your lines will divide the card into four equal-sized sections.

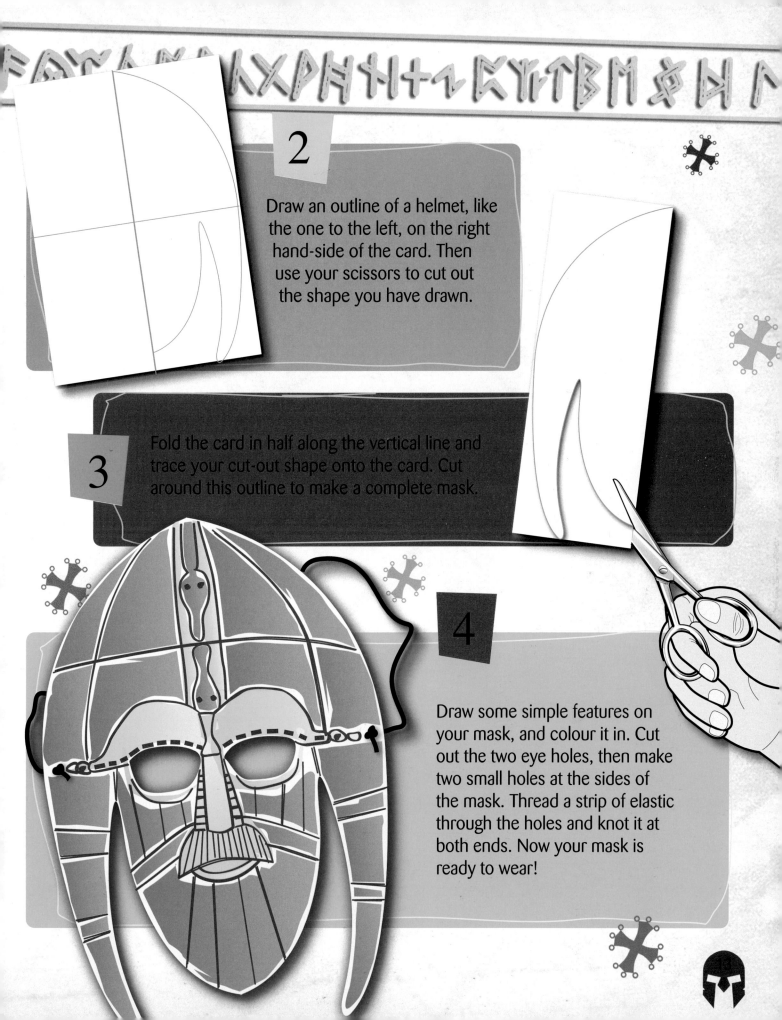

2

Draw an outline of a helmet, like the one to the left, on the right hand-side of the card. Then use your scissors to cut out the shape you have drawn.

3

Fold the card in half along the vertical line and trace your cut-out shape onto the card. Cut around this outline to make a complete mask.

4

Draw some simple features on your mask, and colour it in. Cut out the two eye holes, then make two small holes at the sides of the mask. Thread a strip of elastic through the holes and knot it at both ends. Now your mask is ready to wear!

Anglo-Saxon society

T he king was at the head of Anglo-Saxon society. Then came the nobles, known as thanes, the free people, called churls, and the slaves. After the Anglo-Saxons became Christians, bishops and other members of the Church played an important part in society.

People believed that their king had special powers given by God. This picture from a manuscript shows an English king between the Virgin Mary and Saint Peter.

Ruling England
In the early Anglo-Saxon period, England was split into several kingdoms, but after 937 there was just one king of England. To make the country easier to govern, it was divided into four earldoms. The earldoms were split up into smaller units called shires, and the shires were governed by shire reeves. These important officials later became known as sheriffs.

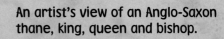

Thanes, churls and slaves

Each village had a thane, who lived in a large hall and owned all the land around the village. Churls worked on the thane's land but also farmed a few strips of land of their own. Slaves did all the hardest jobs and were entirely owned by their masters or mistresses.

An artist's view of an Anglo-Saxon thane, king, queen and bishop.

Men, women and children

Most Anglo-Saxon men worked as farmers or craftsmen, but they also trained as warriors so they could fight for their thane in times of danger. Anglo-Saxon women helped with the farming work and prepared and cooked their family's meals. They also looked after the children and wove cloth which they made into clothes, blankets and hangings. Children worked alongside their parents, learning the skills they would need for adult life.

Some women were skilled at crafts and some worked as musicians, playing harps like the one shown here.

Village life

Most Anglo-Saxon people lived in villages, but by the 1000s some towns had developed, where people gathered to trade. In villages, houses were grouped around the thane's hall and surrounded by farming land. The villagers shared a stone oven for baking bread and a large fire for roasting meat.

Village homes

Churls and their families lived in small houses built from planks of wood, with a steep sloping roof made from straw. Inside, there was a fireplace with a metal cooking pot hanging over it. People stored their possessions in wooden chests and there were strong wooden benches around the walls of the house where the family sat or slept. Most homes had no windows or chimneys, so they were very dark and smoky.

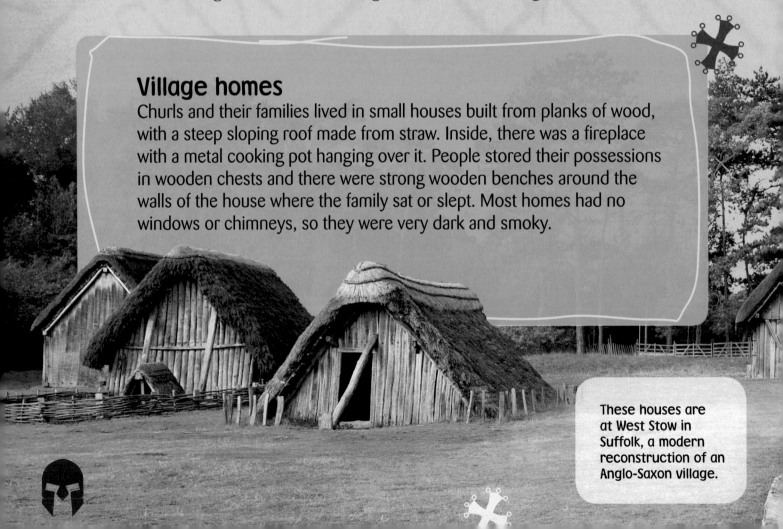

These houses are at West Stow in Suffolk, a modern reconstruction of an Anglo-Saxon village.

Living off the land

The Anglo-Saxons grew crops, such as wheat and oats, and a range of vegetables, including carrots, cabbages, beans and onions. People gathered nuts, berries and fruit, and kept bees for honey. Sheep and cows grazed in the fields, while pigs and chickens stayed closer to the houses.

This picture from an Anglo-Saxon calendar shows farmers ploughing their fields and sowing seed.

Food and feasting

Most Anglo-Saxon people had a daily diet of bread, porridge and vegetable stews. This was sometimes varied with eggs or cheese, or with a small amount of meat or fish. At harvest-time and other special occasions, the thane held a village feast. All the villagers would gather in his hall to eat roast pig and drink ale or mead (a strong drink made from honey).

Village feasts were kept simple, but kings held very grand banquets. This feasting scene is shown in the Bayeux Tapestry (made around 1070).

Religion and belief

The Anglo-Saxon invaders were pagans – people who believed in many gods. But in the 600s, the English people began to convert to Christianity. By the end of the Anglo-Saxon period, almost everyone in England belonged to the Christian Church.

Many gods

The first Anglo-Saxons who arrived in England worshipped many gods and goddesses. Their chief god was Woden, the god of wisdom. Thunor was the god of thunder, Tiw was the god of war, and Frige was the goddess of love. People held open-air ceremonies, and sacrificed animals to their gods in return for their help and protection.

Some Anglo-Saxon gods were very frightening. This is an artist's image of Thunor, the god of thunder.

Christianity arrives

In 597, a monk called Augustine arrived in Kent, in southern England. He had been sent by the Pope (the head of the Church) to convert the Anglo-Saxon people. King Aethelbert of Kent was so impressed by Augustine that he decided to be baptised as a Christian, and he insisted that all his subjects should be baptised too. Augustine set up a monastery at Canterbury which became the centre of the English Church.

King Aethelbert and his wife Queen Bertha both went to hear Augustine preach. Bertha was already a Christian and she helped Augustine to set up his monastery.

Christianity spreads

Augustine was joined by many more monks, and they travelled through southern England, spreading the Christian faith. At the same time, monks from Scotland, Ireland and Wales (where many people were already Christian) were converting the Anglo-Saxons in northwest England. In the 700s, people began building monasteries and convents where monks and nuns could live. By the 900s, the Anglo-Saxons were building village churches.

Some medieval monks produced beautiful illustrated books, known as illuminated manuscripts. This is a page from the Lindisfarne Gospels.

Technology, medicine and magic

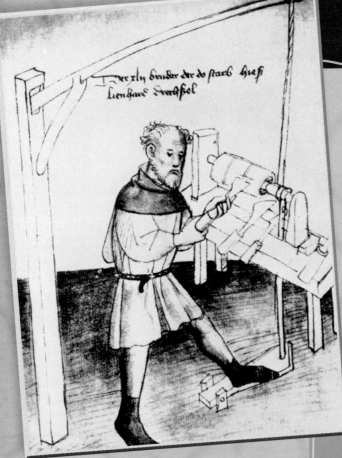

This drawing shows a wood-turner using a pole-lathe.

The Anglo-Saxons were practical people who made simple machines to help them in their work. They used a range of plants to make medicines, but they were also very superstitious and believed in the power of magic.

Technology

People relied on a range of simple technology in their daily lives. Farmers had wooden ploughs that were pulled by oxen and weavers had tall, upright looms for weaving cloth. Wood-turners used a machine called a pole-lathe for carving wood into bowls, plates and cups.

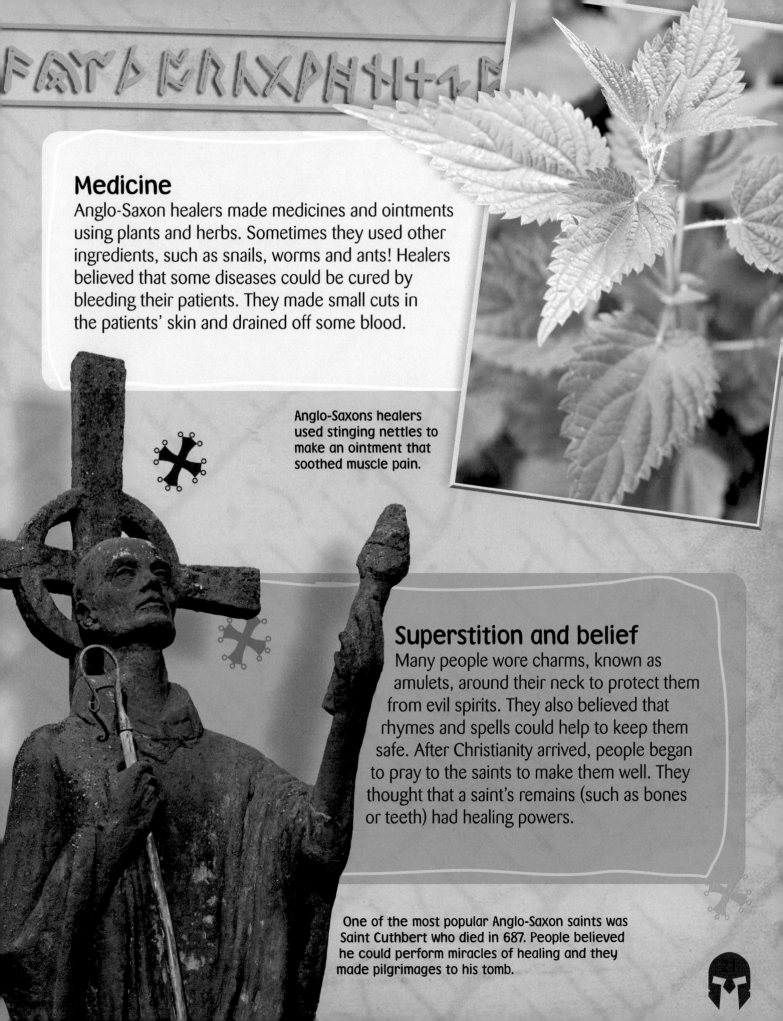

Medicine

Anglo-Saxon healers made medicines and ointments using plants and herbs. Sometimes they used other ingredients, such as snails, worms and ants! Healers believed that some diseases could be cured by bleeding their patients. They made small cuts in the patients' skin and drained off some blood.

Anglo-Saxons healers used stinging nettles to make an ointment that soothed muscle pain.

Superstition and belief

Many people wore charms, known as amulets, around their neck to protect them from evil spirits. They also believed that rhymes and spells could help to keep them safe. After Christianity arrived, people began to pray to the saints to make them well. They thought that a saint's remains (such as bones or teeth) had healing powers.

One of the most popular Anglo-Saxon saints was Saint Cuthbert who died in 687. People believed he could perform miracles of healing and they made pilgrimages to his tomb.

Crafts and music

The Anglo-Saxons were skilled in a wide range of crafts. Each village had a blacksmith and most village women wove their own cloth. By the end of the Anglo-Saxon period, there were also many specialist craftworkers, producing precious objects for the rich.

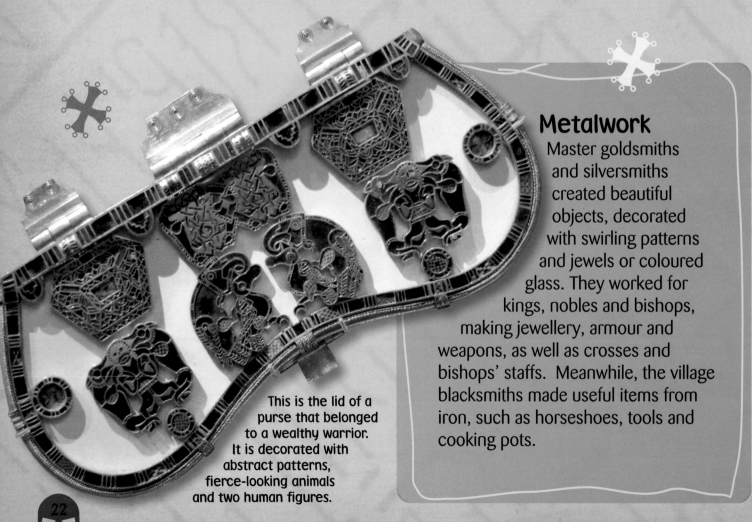

This is the lid of a purse that belonged to a wealthy warrior. It is decorated with abstract patterns, fierce-looking animals and two human figures.

Metalwork

Master goldsmiths and silversmiths created beautiful objects, decorated with swirling patterns and jewels or coloured glass. They worked for kings, nobles and bishops, making jewellery, armour and weapons, as well as crosses and bishops' staffs. Meanwhile, the village blacksmiths made useful items from iron, such as horseshoes, tools and cooking pots.

Carving skills

Anglo-Saxon carvers worked in stone, wood, ivory and bone. They carved figures of people and animals, and created patterns based on natural forms. Skilled ivory carvers made delicately carved objects from walrus tasks and whale bones. Bone from a deer's antlers was used for making everyday objects such as buckles and combs and handles for knives.

You can see the stone-carver's love of pattern in this scene of Saint Michael fighting a dragon.

Making music

Music played a very important part in Anglo-Saxon life. Poets, known as scops, sang songs and played the harp as they told their stories. Some musicians played pipes carved from wood or bone, and some played on instruments made from animal horns.

This manuscript illumination dates from the 700s. It shows King David playing the harp, surrounded by musicians with pipes and horns.

Stories, poems and riddles

M ost people in Anglo-Saxon times couldn't read or write, but they enjoyed sharing stories and they told each other riddles. Some monks wrote about the lives of the saints and recorded the history of their people.

Beowulf has been illustrated many times. In this scene, a monster called Grendel is peering out from behind a tree!

Beowulf

Stories of warriors, giants, monsters and dragons were passed down from one generation to the next, but only a few were written down. The long poem *Beowulf* is the most famous of all the Anglo-Saxon stories. It describes the adventures of a warrior who fights with two monsters and a dragon.

The story of Beowulf was probably told for hundreds of years before it was written down in the 1000s.

A history of England

Much of what we know about the Anglo-Saxons comes from the writings of a monk called Bede, who lived in the 600s. Bede wrote on a wide range of subjects, including religion, science and medicine. His most famous work is *The History of the English Church and People*.

This painting shows Bede with a young scribe, who is writing down his words.

This scene from an ivory casket shows the Anglo-Saxon story of Weland the blacksmith. The symbols carved around the scene are runes.

Runes and riddles

The Anglo-Saxons carved a type of writing, known as runes, on stones and precious objects. People also enjoyed sharing riddles, but their riddles were rather different from the ones we know today. One riddle simply said: 'On the way to a miracle: water becomes bone.' The answer to this riddle was 'Ice'.

The end of the Anglo-Saxons

Between the years 1016 and 1035, England was ruled by a Danish king called Cnut. King Cnut also ruled Denmark, Norway and parts of Sweden, and England became part of a huge Viking Empire.

Edward the Confessor

After Cnut's death, two of his sons, Harold Harefoot and Harthacnut, ruled England. But when Harthacnut died in 1043, there was no obvious Danish leader to take over. The crown returned to the Anglo-Saxon royal family and Edward, the son of Aethelred the Unready, became the next king. Edward became known as Edward the Confessor. He was a devout Christian, but he failed to control the English nobles.

King Edward the Confessor, shown in the Bayeux Tapestry.

HAROLD REX INTERFECTVS

This scene from the Battle of Hastings shows King Harold with an arrow sticking into his eye. You can see his name written above his head.

Rivals for the throne

Edward died in 1066 without an heir to inherit the throne, and Harold Godwinson, the Earl of Wessex, was crowned King of England. But Harold had two rivals– Harald Hardrada, the King of Norway, and William, Duke of Normandy. Soon, King Harold was facing two invasions. Harald attacked from the north while William and the Normans arrived on the south coast.

The Normans take over

King Harold defeated Harald Hardrada, but then he lost his battle against the Normans. King Harold was killed at the Battle of Hastings, and William was crowned the new king of England. The Normans built castles all over England. They introduced new laws and brought the French language to England. Gradually, the Anglo-Saxon way of life died out, although its influence can still be seen today, especially in the English language.

Today, King William I of England is usually known as 'William the Conqueror'.

Facts and figures

Some of our days of the week are named after Anglo-Saxon gods.

- Tuesday comes from Tiw's day
- Wednesday comes from Woden's day
- Thursday comes from Thunor's day
- Friday comes from Frige's day

The Staffordshire Hoard was found in a farmer's field in 2009.

- The hoard consists of over 3,500 items, mostly made from gold.
- Many of the objects in the hoard are related to war, such as helmets and parts of swords.
- The hoard dates from the 600s and 700s.
- The hoard was probably buried at a time of danger with the intention of rescuing it later.

The Sutton Hoo ship burial was uncovered near the Suffolk coast in 1939.

- Inside a mound was a wooden ship, measuring 27 metres long, with a central burial chamber.
- The burial chamber probably contained the body of Raedwald, King of the East Angles.
- Inside the burial chamber were the warrior's possessions, including a helmet and sword.
- The burial probably took place in the 600s.

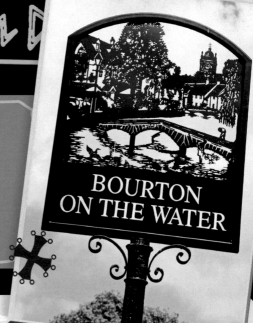

Many English villages and towns have Anglo-Saxon names. Place names ending in 'ton' or 'ham' were Anglo-Saxon villages. The ending 'barrow' meant a wood and 'stow' was a meeting place.

BOURTON ON THE WATER

Timeline

43CE The Romans invade Britain and it becomes part of the Roman Empire.

380s Angles, Saxons and Jutes launch raids on England.

410 The last Roman soldiers leave Britain.

550s The Angles, Saxons and Jutes set up kingdoms in England.

597 Augustine starts converting the Anglo-Saxons to Christianity.

790s The Vikings carry out raids on England.

878 King Alfred defeats the Danes at the Battle of Edington.

937 King Aethelstan defeats the Danes at the Battle of Brunanburh. He becomes the first king of a united England.

991 King Aethelred starts paying Danegeld to the Danes.

1013 King Sweyn Forkbeard of Denmark conquers England.

1016 Cnut becomes king of England. He reigns for 19 years.

1042 Edward the Confessor becomes king of England.

1066 The Normans win the Battle of Hastings and William is crowned King of England. The Anglo-Saxon age comes to an end.

Glossary

abstract Based on ideas rather than figures and objects.

archaeologist Someone who learns about the past by digging up old objects and buildings.

baptise To perform a ceremony that shows you have become a member of a religion. In Christianity, water is poured on a person's head during baptism.

CE The letters CE stand for 'common era'. They refer to dates after the birth of Christ.

ceremony Special religious events or services.

churl A free man or woman. Churls usually worked on a thane's land.

convert To persuade someone to join a religion.

Danes People who come from Denmark.

descendants People belonging to later generations who all share the same ancestor.

devout Deeply religious.

evidence Objects and information that help to prove something.

fictional Made up or invented.

generation All the people born around the same time.

illumination A picture or some decoration added to a hand-written book.

ingredient One of the items that something is made from.

invaders Warriors from abroad who attack a country with the plan of taking it over.

invasion An attack on a country by warriors from abroad.

manuscript A hand-written book.

raid A sudden attack on a place.

sacrifice To kill an animal or a person as an offering to a god.

scribe Someone who writes out books by hand.

source Something that provides information.

staff A thick stick, often used as a symbol of power.

superstitious Believing in ideas that are not based on fact or reason.

symbol A shape or object that represents something else.

technology The use of science to do practical things.

thane A nobleman or woman. Thanes owned land and usually lived in a large hall.

Further reading

The Best and Worst Jobs: Anglo-Saxon and Viking times, Clive Gifford (Wayland, 2015)
The History Detective Investigates: Anglo-Saxons, Neil Tonge (Wayland, 2014)
Men, Women and Children: in Anglo-Saxon times, Jane Bingham (Wayland, 2011)
What they don't tell you about: Anglo-Saxons, Robert Fowke (Wayland, 2014)

Websites

http://www.bbc.co.uk/schools/primaryhistory/anglo_saxons/
An interactive guide to Anglo-Saxon life, with sections on growing up, stories and pastimes and Anglo-Saxon beliefs. Includes an archaeology game called 'Dig it up'.

http://www.britishmuseum.org/explore/young_explorers/childrens_online_tours/ anglo-saxon_england/anglo-saxon_england.aspx
An illustrated guide to the Anglo-Saxons based on objects from the British Museum. The objects include the Sutton Hoo helmet, a drinking horn, a necklace and a carved ship's prow. Includes an Anglo-Saxon recipe for chicken stew.

http://anglosaxondiscovery.ashmolean.org/index.html
A children's guide to Anglo-Saxon life produced by the Ashmolean Musuem, Oxford. There are sections on the arrival of the Anglo-Saxons, Anglo-Saxon life and death and kings and kingdoms.

Index